A History of
West Virginia

A History of
West Virginia

by Anna Egan Smucker

Edited and produced by
Therese M. Hess

for the

West
Virginia
Humanities
Council

Originally published as a reading text, this little book has been used to help thousands of West Virginia adults learn to read. In the meantime, it discovered a second life as a popular introduction to our state's history for readers of all ages and every level of education. We are proud to make *A History of West Virginia* available for the general market, and we again acknowledge the support of Ashland Foundation and Verizon for earlier editions of this book.

The West Virginia Humanities Council, a nonprofit corporation, works every day to promulgate the humanities in West Virginia, including the story of our rich Mountain State heritage. You may contact us at

West Virginia Humanities Council
1310 Kanawha Boulevard, East
Charleston, West Virginia 25301
304-346-8500
www.wvhumanities.org

Contributions to the West Virginia Humanities Council
are tax deductible.

Cover photograph by Steve Shaluta, Jr.
West Virginia Division of Tourism

ISBN 1-891852-39-6

Reprinted with permission by Quarrier Press, Charleston, WV
www.wvbookco.com

Contents

Note of Thanks

I would like to thank the West Virginia Humanities Council for funding this project. Much of the material in this history is taken from *West Virginia – A Film History*. My thanks to the writers Mark Samels and John Alexander Williams.

Other information came from these publications:
- *Goldenseal*, Vol. 21, No. 3.
- Otis K. Rice and Stephen W. Brown, *West Virginia: A History*, Second Edition, Lexington, KY: University Press of Kentucky, 1993.
- John C. Waugh, *The Class of 1846*. New York, NY: Warner Books, 1994.
- John Alexander Williams, *West Virginia: A History for Beginners*. Charleston, WV: Appalachian Editions, 1993.

I would also like to thank Jack Sandy Anderson, Katherine Jourdan, Virginia Kucan, and Dr. Thomasina Redd for sharing their West Virginia stories with me. Thanks to Ashland, Inc. Foundation and Verizon for their previous financial assistance with this book. I would like to thank David Houchin and Thomas W. Dixon, Jr., for help with research; Bruce Blankenship, Patricia Harris, and Linn Maxwell for their computer help; Cheryl Ware and Ken Sullivan for reading the manuscript and making suggestions; and Therese Hess for her fine work as editor. Any remaining mistakes in this book are my own.

Finally, I owe many thanks to the friends and family who are so supportive of this writer.

Anna Egan Smucker

Introduction

In 1671, an English explorer stood at the top of a Virginia mountain. He looked out over the rugged land that would someday be part of West Virginia. The mountains seemed to go on forever. They looked like giant ocean waves. To this explorer, whose name was Robert Fallam, the mountains were beautiful. They were also, in many ways, frightening. How could anyone ever travel across them, he must have wondered.

The mountains *were* hard to cross. They cut western Virginia off from the eastern part of Virginia, and from the rest of the country. The mountains were one reason why, in the 1860s, western Virginia broke away from Virginia and became the state of West Virginia.

The history of West Virginia is a story of struggle—of white settlers against the Native Americans, of neighbor against neighbor in the Civil War, of coal miners fighting for fair pay and a safe workplace.

The history of West Virginia is also the story of a place whose hills and hollows are a part of its people, a place where family has always been important. It is the story of people proud to call this beautiful, rugged land home.

CHAPTER 1

An Important Hunting Ground

The Early Hunters

Long before the first white explorers came to what is now West Virginia, early people, known as the "Early Hunters," were here. Around 13,000 years ago they hunted herds of animals such as the mastodon and other large animals that are now gone forever.

We know these people hunted around the Ohio River. We have found some of their spear points.

Between 6,000 and 11,000 years ago, another group of early people began to settle along the Ohio and Kanawha (Ka-NA-wa) Rivers. These people gathered wild food,

Spear points like these were found in areas around the Ohio River.

fished, and hunted. They left piles of bones, shells, and seeds at the places where they stayed. From these we can tell they ate fish, shellfish, wild fruit, and nuts.

The Mound Builders

The early people were followed by the "Mound Builders." The mounds they built were special burial

places. The most famous mound is the Grave Creek Mound in what is now Moundsville. It was built more than 2,000 years ago. It is the largest mound of its kind in the United States. Not all of the early people built mounds. Some began to plant seeds for food. One of their main crops was sunflowers.

The Grave Creek Mound in Moundsville, Marhall County.

Moundsville, Marshall County

The next people in this area were still hunters and gatherers of food, but farming was becoming more important. They grew corn. Some of them also built mounds. Many of their mounds can still be seen in the Kanawha Valley. These mounds were not as big as the ones built by the earlier "Mound Builders."

Native Americans

Beginning around 1,000 years ago, another group of early people began living in villages. They surrounded their villages with pointed logs stuck in the ground. They grew squash and beans as well as corn. They hunted and fished. The Native Americans (Indians) who were in this area when the white people arrived came from these early peoples. Few Native Americans lived here when the white people first began to explore and settle this area. There were some hunting camps and villages. Most often, explorers found untended fields and empty villages. In one place, they found a field of corn still growing.

We do not know for sure what happened to these Native Americans. Some believe they died of sicknesses brought to this country by the white people. Measles and smallpox killed thousands of Native Americans.

Others believe they were driven from their villages by the powerful Iroquois (EAR-a-kwoi). The Iroquois Confederacy was the largest and strongest of the Indian groups who claimed the area of western Virginia.[*]

[*] In this book, "western Virginia" is used to refer to the area of Virginia that became the state of West Virginia in 1863.

CHAPTER 2

Claiming the Land

First White Explorers

Explorers were the first white people who came into the area that is now West Virginia. In 1671, the English explorers Thomas Batts and Robert Fallam reached the New River. They claimed it, and all the land drained by it, for England.

In 1716, Alexander Spotswood, a Royal Governor of Virginia, led a group of explorers across the Blue Ridge Mountains and into the Shenandoah Valley. When they started their trip, they must have looked like they were going on a picnic. They wore fancy clothes. They were loaded down with good things to eat and drink. Along the way, hornets stung the horses. One horse was bitten by a rattlesnake. Two men got the measles. Everyone's fine clothes were torn.

Finally, Spotswood and his men reached the Shenandoah Valley. They saw it was a land rich in timber and grass for grazing animals. They claimed it for the King of England. Spotswood gave each gentleman a little golden horseshoe. The group became known as the "Knights of the Golden Horseshoe." Their exploring opened the area to settlers.

First White Settlers

In 1722, a treaty was signed between the Iroquois and the Virginia government. This allowed Virginians to settle in the valleys between the Blue Ridge Mountains and the highest ridge of the Allegheny (Al-a-GAY-nee) Mountains.

Shepherdstown, Jefferson County

We cannot be sure who first settled the area. A man named Morgan Morgan is often called the first white settler in what is now West Virginia. As early as 1727, a group of Germans settled at New Mecklenburg. Today it is called Shepherdstown.

The Governor of the Royal Colony of Virginia encouraged people to settle in this land between the mountains. Many did. They came from the colonies of Pennsylvania and New Jersey. Many came from northern Ireland and Germany. Others came from Scotland and Wales. By 1750, much of the land between the mountains was settled. People began to look toward the land west of the Allegheny Mountains as a possible place to live.

Too Many "Owners"

In the 1740s, Virginia had made another treaty with the Iroquois. The white people thought it gave them the right to make settlements all the way to the Ohio River. But the Iroquois did not own the land they sold to the white people.

Settlement of this land proved to be as dangerous as trying to make a home on a battleground—because the French, the English, and the Shawnee all claimed to own it.

꧁꧂

CHAPTER 3

The French and Indian War

France Claims Ohio Valley

France was not ready to give up its claim to the area that is now West Virginia. In 1749, the French buried lead plates at the mouths of all the major streams flowing into the Ohio River. The writing on these plates said that all the land drained by the Ohio River belonged to the King of France. This included most of western Virginia.

The French began to build forts to protect their claim. They built an important fort where the Ohio River begins. They called it Fort Duquesne (Du-KANE). This is where Pittsburgh now stands.

English Fight French and Indians

At that time, George Washington was a young man. He led a group of Virginia soldiers in two battles against the French. He won the first battle. He lost the second. He and his men were taken prisoner. They were sent back to

Virginia with a message from the French. The message ordered the English to stay out of the Ohio Valley. Most of the Native Americans decided to fight on the side of the French. They thought the French would win the war.

In 1755, the English sent General Braddock and 1,400 British troops to aid the Virginians. General Braddock had spent 50 years in the British Army. He was used to fighting with soldiers lined up in rows. His soldiers wore red and white uniforms. They marched to the beat of battle drums. This style of fighting made them easy targets.

About 10 miles from Fort Duquesne, the French and Native Americans attacked Braddock's army. They shot at the British soldiers from behind trees and rocks. They defeated Braddock's army. Braddock was wounded. He died a few days later.

Settlers Live in Fear

This defeat struck fear in the settlers who had moved into the area between the Allegheny Mountains and the Ohio River. They had hoped the British Army would save them. Now they knew they were on their own. They would have to try to protect themselves.

This battle was part of a nine-year war between England and France that was fought in many parts of the world. In America, it was called the French and Indian War.

The defeat of General Braddock left the settlers open

to attacks. Almost all of the settlements in the New River, Greenbrier (GREEN-bry-er), and Monongahela (Ma-non-ga-HE-la) areas were destroyed. Many settlers moved back across the mountains into the safer area of the Shenandoah Valley.

George Washington was now in charge of all of the Virginia soldiers. He almost gave up his command. He knew he would not be able to protect the settlers.

Rugged Land Makes Fighting Harder

In February of 1756, the Governor of Virginia sent soldiers to attack the Shawnee villages in Ohio. The Governor did not know how rugged the land was. It rained for days. The creeks and rivers were overflowing their banks. The men had to cross the flooded Big Sandy River 66 times in the span of 15 miles. Rain turned to snow. Starving packhorses were left behind. There was only a little bit of flour left for food, and hunters could find no wild animals. Many men deserted. Finally the officers voted to return home. This would not be the last time that the rugged land of western Virginia caused problems for soldiers.

The Native Americans continued their attacks. They attacked forts, but mostly they attacked the settlers who lived far apart from one another.

England Finally Wins

In 1757, British soldiers won major victories against the French. In 1758, General Forbes led 6,000 British soldiers against the French at Fort Duquesne. The French commander knew his soldiers were outnumbered. He ordered his men to blow up the fort and retreat north toward Canada. In the Ohio Valley, many Native Americans who had fought for the French now made peace with the British.

CHAPTER 4

Native Americans Fight for Their Land

The Treaty of Paris was signed in 1763. It ended the war
between England and France. All of the Ohio Valley lands
claimed by the French were given to the English. The Royal
Colony of Virginia set aside some of this land to pay soldiers who had fought in the war. Officers could each claim
5,000 acres of the set-aside land. Privates could select 50
acres. But it was still not safe for white people to settle in
western Virginia. Native Americans, especially the
Shawnee, still claimed the land.

Natives Need Hunting Ground

This land of western Virginia was an important hunting ground for the Native Americans. The animals they
hunted gave them food. They made their clothing from
the skins of the animals. Then white traders came into the
area looking for furs. The traders wanted the pelts of bea-

ver, mink, and fox. The Native Americans wanted guns, ammunition, tools, cloth, and alcohol from the white traders. The Native Americans needed to hunt now more than ever. They needed to hunt not only for food, but to have pelts to trade for the new things they wanted.

Settlers Destroy Hunting Ground

At first, the Native Americans were friendly toward the few white people who came into the area. The first settlers built small cabins. These were often no larger than 10 by 20 square feet. Some settlers lived in caves or large hollow trees until they could build cabins. When more white people came, the Native Americans watched them chop down trees to build houses. Then the white settlers began to burn the tall oak, poplar, and walnut trees to clear the land for their crops. The Native Americans saw their hunting grounds being destroyed. They wanted to stop it.

A Bitter Time for Everyone

At the conclusion of the French and Indian War in 1763, Native Americans led by Chief Pontiac (PON-tee-ack) once again attacked forts and settlements. Hundreds were killed. To stop the killing, the King of England ordered settlers not to go west of the Allegheny Mountains. It was too late. People poured into the area in search of new land to settle. The Native Americans attacked them again and again. The settlers fought back, raiding Native American camps. It was a bitter time. Many people on both sides vowed to spend the rest of their lives attacking those who had killed their loved ones. Women, children, the sick, and the old of both the Native Americans and the white settlers were murdered. No one was safe.

A Mingo chief, known to white people as Chief Logan, was friendly toward the white settlers until one night in April of 1774. On that night, a group of settlers invited eight Native Americans to come drink with them. It was a cruel trick. The whites killed the Native Americans and cut up their bodies. An unborn baby was cut out of its mother and scalped. A brother and sister of Chief Logan were among those killed.

Chief Logan vowed revenge. He led attacks on many settlements. He killed 13 whites before he returned to his village. Later, when he was asked to sign a treaty with the British, he refused. This is what he said:

"I appeal to any white man to say if ever he entered Logan's cabin hungry, and he gave him not meat; if ever he came cold and naked, and he clothed him not....I had even thought to have lived with you but for the injuries of one man ... [who] in cold blood...murdered all the relations of Logan not even sparing my women and children....Who is there to mourn for Logan? Not one."

Chief Logan

Treaty Gives Land to Settlers

Native Americans, especially the Shawnee, continued their attacks. The settlers fought back. Lord Dunmore was now the Royal Governor of Virginia. He organized an army of western Virginians to attack the Native Americans. The Virginians under the command of Andrew Lewis defeated Shawnee Chief Cornstalk in a bloody battle at Point Pleasant in 1774. A treaty was signed by Governor Dunmore and the Shawnee, Delaware, and Mingo tribes. The Native Americans gave up their claim to all land south of the Ohio River. This included the area that is now West Virginia. The treaty was made final in 1775.

Point Pleasant, Mason County

CHAPTER 5

The Revolutionary War

Colonies Fight for Independence

By the late 1770s, many Americans were tired of being ruled by the British. The colonies began fighting to be free of England. Many men in western Virginia joined the army to fight the British. We call this struggle the "Revolutionary War" or the "War for Independence." Not many young men were left to guard the settlements.

Settlers Battle British and Indians

The British gave guns and bullets to the Native Americans. They wanted them to attack the settlers. In 1777, only two years after signing the peace treaty, the Shawnee, Mingo, and Wyandot (WHY-an-dot) tribes attacked the settlers who remained in western Virginia. The year 1777 became known as the "bloody year of the three sevens."

Chief Cornstalk had become a peacemaker between

the tribes and the white settlers. He came to the fort at Point Pleasant to warn the settlers that he could no longer keep the Shawnee from attacking them. He and his son were taken prisoner and held in the fort. When Native Americans killed two white men near the fort, angry soldiers killed Cornstalk and his son. Five white men were charged with the murders. They were set free when no one would testify against them.

Fort Henry in 1777, located at what is now the city of Wheeling.

Raids and battles continued. On August 31, 1777, Native Americans attacked Fort Henry on Wheeling Creek. The fort held out for three days but almost half its men were killed. Native Americans attacked settlements and smaller forts along the Greenbrier, Monongahela, and Ohio Rivers.

In September 1782, Fort Henry was attacked again. Ammunition inside the fort was almost gone. According to legend, a 16-year-old girl named Betty Zane saved the fort by running for gunpowder as bullets whizzed around her. This second battle of Fort Henry was the last big battle against the Native Americans in western Virginia.

Settlers Win, Become a Free Nation

East of the mountains, the British surrendered to the Americans led by George Washington in October 1782 at the Battle of Yorktown. The Revolutionary War was over. The settlers were no longer English colonists. They were Americans. A peace treaty was signed between England and the United States. England gave up claim to the land south of Canada and east of the Mississippi River.

After the war, thousands of settlers came over the mountains. In 1794, President George Washington sent 3,000 soldiers to make the land west of the mountains safe from attacks by Native Americans. Led by General Anthony Wayne, they defeated the Native Americans in Ohio at the Battle of Fallen Timbers. The Shawnee left their burned villages and moved farther west. The land which was to become West Virginia was now open to white settlers.

CHAPTER 6

Farms, Towns, and Industries

Owning Land

Who owned the land? Often, many people claimed the same plots of land in western Virginia. This was a problem for people who wanted to own the land they lived on. The same land could have been claimed by the first settlers, then given to soldiers as part of their pay for serving in the French and Indian War. Many soldiers sold their land to speculators. Speculators hoped to get rich by buying a lot of land for little money. They hoped to sell the land later and make a profit.

Most speculators lived outside the mountains of western Virginia. They hired surveyors to mark off their land. Many of these surveyors did not do a good job. Sometimes the stones or trees they used as markers were removed. During most of the 1800s, lawyers were kept busy trying to figure out who owned what land. Because of this confusion, many people moved farther west. There, they could be more sure that the land they bought would be their own.

Building Towns

Nevertheless, throughout the 1800s the population of western Virginia grew. Settlements became towns. New counties were formed. Roads were built. Ferry boats began business at important river crossings. Farms were started. Some were large but, because of the rugged land, most were small. Farmers grew the crops and raised the animals they needed to supply food for their families. Any extra was taken to market. It was sold to buy the things the farmer was not able to grow or make for himself.

The Whiskey Rebellion

Many farmers in western Virginia found that it was easier to ship their extra corn to market if they made it into corn whiskey. The whiskey also sold for a much higher price than bushels of corn. When the government put a tax on whiskey, farmers became angry. In 1794, some farmers in Monongalia County forced a tax collector to leave. They joined Pennsylvania farmers in this struggle against the government which became known as the Whiskey Rebellion. Government troops were sent in to enforce the law and the rebellion ended.

Monongalia County

However, many farmers continued to believe they had the right to make and sell whiskey without being taxed.

Travel by Road and River

Good roads were necessary for trade to grow. The National Road, also called the Cumberland Road, was completed from Cumberland to Wheeling in 1818. In the 1830s the Northwestern Turnpike was built to connect Winchester and Parkersburg. Other roads crossed the southern area of western Virginia. The roads were filled with people traveling on foot, horseback, and in stagecoaches. The roads were also filled with cattle, hogs, and sheep being driven to market. Inns, taverns, and hotels were built along the roads. Towns along the roads grew in size.

Rivers were important for transportation of people and goods but, during many times of the year, the water levels were too low for boat traffic. Locks and dams had to be built on some of the rivers to raise the water level for the new steamboats.

Many New Industries

Salt-making was one of the first industries to develop in western Virginia. Saltwater, or brine, was boiled to make salt in the Kanawha Valley.

Iron was manufactured along the Ohio and

Monongahela Rivers and in the Shenandoah Valley. The iron was made into such things as nails, plows, and barrel

The salt works in Malden, Kanawha County.

hoops to meet the needs of the settlers. There was one last struggle with England, called the War of 1812. No battles were fought in western Virginia, but Peter Tarr's iron furnace, near what is now the city of Weirton, made cannonballs that were used in that war. Other weapons were made in Harpers Ferry.

Weirton, Hancock County

Mills that used water power to grind wheat into flour were built in the northern and eastern areas of western Virginia. Pottery and glass factories made dishes, bottles, and glass for windows. Other factories made wool and cotton into cloth. Sawmills cut boards for houses, boats, furniture, and barrels.

Sending Goods to Eastern Markets

If the industries of western Virginia were going to develop as fast as they were in other states, more and better methods of transportation were necessary. There was still no fast way for western Virginians to send goods to markets in the East.

Other states were building canals and railroads. In the 1820s, the Virginia government cut off funds for a canal that would have crossed the mountains into western Virginia. Eastern Virginians had fairly good roads and rivers. They did not want to pay for a canal or other western improvements that would raise their taxes. Many people in western Virginia felt that eastern Virginia was not interested in helping them develop their industries and resources.

CHAPTER 7

The Split Begins

In many ways, western Virginia and eastern Virginia had been growing apart ever since the first settlements were founded west of the mountains. When western Virginia split from eastern Virginia, it was not a sudden event. It was the result of many differences that built up over the years.

Background Differences

Many of the settlers who came over the mountains after the Revolutionary War did not come from the eastern part of Virginia. They came from Pennsylvania, New Jersey, New England, and New York. Some came from England, Ireland, Scotland, and Wales. Many settlers in the northern part of eastern Virginia were German and Scotch-Irish. Many of these settlers had no attachment to eastern Virginia.

Land Differences

The land itself made western Virginia different from eastern Virginia. East of the mountains, much of the land was rich and flat. It was suitable for large farms. The main crop was tobacco. Large landowners used slaves to work this crop. Most of the tobacco was shipped down eastern Virginia's rivers and then across the ocean to markets in Europe.

Western Virginia was rich in natural resources: iron, coal, natural gas, oil, timber, and salt. As these industries grew, western Virginia became more different than ever from eastern Virginia which depended on its large tobacco farms and slave labor.

Political Differences

Other differences were political. People in the two areas had different ideas about who should be able to vote. According to the Virginia constitution, only white men who owned land were allowed to vote. Most people in western Virginia felt this gave too much power to the rich landowners. More landowners lived in eastern Virginia than in western Virginia.

Also, many government officials were chosen by other government officials. Most western Virginians thought government officials should be elected. Eastern Virginia had many more representatives in state government than did western Virginia. Western Virginians did not think this was fair.

Western Virginians Want Change

In 1829-1830, a convention was held in Richmond. The convention rejected the changes the western Virginians wanted. Wheeling newspapers began to call for western Virginia to separate from eastern Virginia.

Lewisburg, Greenbrier County

In 1842, leaders of western Virginia met in Lewisburg to demand changes in the Virginia constitution. They also demanded improvements in transportation. The government in Richmond ignored their demands.

At a convention held in Richmond in 1850, western Virginians finally won more political power. All white men over the age of 21 could now vote. Many political officials who had been appointed now had to be elected. For the first time, the governor of Virginia was from western Virginia. He was Joseph Johnson from Harrison County.

Transportation improvements were made in western Virginia. The Baltimore and Ohio Railroad was built over the Allegheny Mountains. In 1852, the B&O, as the railroad was called, reached Wheeling. The railroad opened up western Virginia more than the roads ever had.

Harrison County

Leaders in both eastern and western Virginia seemed more willing to try to work things out. But, at the same time, the country itself was being pulled into two separate parts—the North and the South. Virginia was on the border. It was a mix of both North and South.

CHAPTER 8

The Civil War

Slavery

On the eastern side of the mountains, thousands of slaves worked on the big Virginia farms that were called plantations. There were fewer slaves in western Virginia. These had been brought over the mountains by Virginia farmers.

Farms on the west side of the mountains were much smaller than the farms on the eastern side. On the small farms in western Virginia there were not many slaves. Often, farmers and slaves worked together in the fields. But a slave was still a slave and not a free person. Runaway slaves were often whipped in public. Families were split up as members were sold to different owners. In the saltworks of the Kanawha Valley, slaves were treated as if they were animals.

John Brown

More and more people opposed slavery as time passed. There were slave rebellions, one led by Nat Turner in eastern Virginia in 1831. Later, a man named John Brown began to work on a plan to wipe out slavery. He was willing to use violence to do it.

In 1856, Brown and four of his sons attacked and killed five pro-slavery settlers in Kansas. In 1857, Brown started gathering weapons for his battle to free the slaves.

John Brown

In 1859, he moved to a farm in Maryland that was near Harpers Ferry. On October 16, 1859, Brown and his followers took control of the government's guns at the arsenal in Harpers Ferry. Brown planned to give the guns he captured to slaves. He thought if slaves had guns they would rise up against their owners. During the raid, two of Brown's sons and many of his followers were killed. Brown was captured. On December 2, 1859, he was hanged.

After his death, Brown became a hero to many people who were against slavery. His actions and his death widened the split between those who approved of slavery and those who did not.

North and South Disagree About Slavery

The North and the South were becoming more and more divided over the issues of slavery and the rights of states to decide matters for themselves. In November 1860, Abraham Lincoln was elected the 16th president of the United States. Leaders in the southern states were afraid that he would do away with slavery.

One month after Lincoln's election, South Carolina separated from the Union. Six other states followed. Virginia tried to decide which way to go.

War Begins; Virginians on Both Sides

On April 12, 1861, near Charleston, South Carolina, Confederate guns fired on Fort Sumter. The Civil War had begun. Now Virginia had to decide whether to stay in the Union or join other Southern states in the new government that called itself the Confederate States of America.

John Carlile of Clarksburg led the fight to keep Virginia in the Union. Waitman Willey of Morgantown, who had freed his own slaves, warned that Virginia would break apart if it left the Union.

On April 17, 1861, Virginia delegates voted 88 to 55 to join the Confederacy. Most of the delegates from northwestern Virginia voted to stay with the Union. Fighting between Virginia's northern and southern troops began within a month.

"The Philippi Races"

Both the Union and the Confederacy wanted to control the B&O Railroad that ran through western Virginia. In May, Colonel George Porterfield and his Confederate soldiers had control of Grafton. Grafton was an important railroad center on the B&O. Union General George McClellan sent troops from Ohio. He ordered Colonel Benjamin Kelley to retake Grafton. Porterfield knew that he did not have enough men to stand and fight. After burning two railroad bridges, he retreated to Philippi (FILL-a-pee).

Early on the dark rainy morning of June 2, 1861, Union forces began a surprise attack. The weather was so bad the Confederates had no one standing watch. They were all asleep in their camp. At the sound of the cannons, the Confederate soldiers jumped out of their bedrolls. They ran to save their lives. Many were still in their underwear. The battle was called "The Philippi Races."

Grafton,
Taylor County

Phillipi,
Barbour County

"Stonewall" Jackson

Meanwhile, Confederate Colonel Thomas Jackson was in Harpers Ferry. He was busy capturing locomotives and railroad cars to send south for use by the Confederate soldiers. Jackson sent four locomotives down the rails to Winchester, Virginia, where the tracks ended. From there, teams of horses dragged the locomotives over 20 miles of road to Strasburg, Virginia. There they were put back on the railroad.

Around mid-June, the Union army was near Harpers Ferry. When Jackson was ordered to retreat, he blew up the railroad bridges. He set fire to what was left of the cars and locomotives. He didn't want them to be of any use to the Union Soldiers.

WV State Archives

Thomas "Stonewall" Jackson

The Civil War's first large battle was the Battle of Bull Run. It was fought near Manassas, Virginia. At first it looked as if the Union soldiers were going to win. They were stopped by a group of Southern soldiers under Jackson's command who stood "like a stone wall" in their way. The Confederates won the battle. Jackson was known from that day on as "Stonewall" Jackson.

Moving Toward Statehood

The fighting grew worse. Wheeling newspaper

editor Archibald Campbell wrote that a new state should be formed in western Virginia. He said that the new state should be free of slaves. Many people agreed with him. About three times as many western Virginians were fighting for the Union as were fighting for the Confederacy.

In July of 1861, Union soldiers won an important victory at Rich Mountain in Randolph County. In September, Union troops defeated the Confederates at Gauley River. Union soldiers now controlled all of northwestern Virginia, most of the Kanawha Valley, and the B&O Railroad. Confederates still held the Greenbrier and other southeastern valleys.

Confederates who were camped in the mountains had trouble getting food and supplies. It rained constantly. Wagons got stuck in the mud. Soldiers suffered from pneumonia, measles, and mumps. Confederate General Robert E. Lee gave up his plans to attack the B&O and to win back the Kanawha Valley.

By the end of 1861, Union soldiers were in control of most of western Virginia. The way was clear for the forming of a new state.

CHAPTER 9

A New State

It was not easy to make a new state from part of an old state. It took many legal steps.

Wheeling, Ohio County

On May 11, 1861, western Virginians who wanted to stay in the Union met in Wheeling. They decided an election should be held so that voters of western Virginia could make their wishes known. On May 23, 1861, most voters voted in favor of the Union.

A New Government

On July 13, 1861, the Second Wheeling Convention was held. Delegates voted to form a new Virginia government. It was called the Reorganized Government of Virginia. It was loyal to the Union.

Francis H. Pierpont of Marion County was elected Governor of the Reorganized Government. John Carlile and Waitman Willey, the men who had led the fight to keep Virginia in the Union, were chosen to be the new government's senators in the U.S. Congress.

All of this allowed a new state to be formed within the borders of the old state of Virginia. In an election held in October 1861, voters approved the creation of this new state.

A New Name

In November 1861, another convention was held in Wheeling. Delegates wrote a constitution for the new state. Also, the new state needed a name. Many names were suggested. New Virginia, Allegheny, and Kanawha were some of them. Finally the name West Virginia was chosen. Most people wanted the entire B&O Railroad line to be in the new state. That is why the counties in the northeast part of Virginia were included, even though they were more sympathetic to the Confederacy than to the Union.

The Issue of Slavery

On May 29, 1862, Senator Willey presented West Virginia's application for statehood to the U.S. Senate. Congress said that slavery had to be outlawed in the state. Willey proposed an amendment that would, over time, do away with slavery in West Virginia. The Senate passed the bill with the amendment attached. Then the U.S. House of Representatives passed it. Now it was up to President Lincoln to sign the bill that would create the new state of West Virginia.

Lincoln Must Decide

Lincoln was worried. The Constitution of the United States clearly said that no state could be divided against its will. While Lincoln thought about what to do, Archibald Campbell, the editor of a newspaper called the *Wheeling Intelligencer*, wrote a letter to try to persuade the President. Governor Pierpont threatened to resign if Lincoln vetoed the bill.

Half of Lincoln's cabinet was in favor of the new state. Half was against it. This was a time of war. Lincoln felt that West Virginia could do more good in the Union than outside it. On December 31, 1862, he signed the bill.

West Virginia Becomes a State

Lincoln then issued a proclamation stating that West Virginia would become the 35th state on June 20, 1863. On that date, West Virginia became the 35th star in the American flag. Arthur H. Boreman of Parkersburg became

Statue of Abraham Lincoln on the State Capitol grounds in Charleston.

the first governor of the new state of West Virginia.

Fighting Continues

The Civil War was still far from over. In West Virginia, Union soldiers had only shaky control. Confederates called "bushwhackers" struck fear in people who supported the Union. Bushwhackers were more horse thieves and criminals than they were soldiers. They beheaded a Union message carrier. People were often shot to settle past family or neighborhood fights that had nothing to do with the war.

Large armies were of no use against the bushwhackers. In West Virginia's rugged land, a few dozen sharpshooters at a steep place in the mountains could hold off hundreds of soldiers.

Union General Robert Milroy was so frustrated by the bushwhackers that he ordered people who supported the Confederates to pay for the property the bushwhackers stole or destroyed. If they refused, he said, their houses would be burned and they would be shot. Milroy later canceled the order. Union soldiers controlled most of the towns. Soldiers on both sides took what they needed wherever they could find it.

Women's War Roles

Women, children, and older men were left to take care of the farms. They lived in constant fear of raids by bushwhackers. Anna Jarvis of Grafton started a work club to provide food and medicine to women who had lost everything because of the war.

Women worked as spies for both the Union and the Confederacy. Belle Boyd of Martinsburg charmed Union generals into telling important military secrets that she passed on to the Confederacy. She was arrested seven times. Nancy Hart Douglas, who lived in the Summersville area, became a member of the Moccasin (MOCK-a-sin) Rangers when her brother-in-law was killed by Union soldiers. She passed Union plans on to the Confederates. After escaping from prison in Summersville, she led the Confederates in burning the town.

Martinsburg, Berkeley County

Summersville, Nicholas County

Stonewall Jackson Dies

On May 2, 1863, Stonewall Jackson was shot by his own men. In the darkness, they had mistaken him for a Union soldier. He died eight days later. The Confederacy lost one of its greatest generals. Although Jackson remained loyal to Virginia, this Clarksburg native is honored as one of West Virginia's heroes. No general was better than Jackson at moving his troops quickly and surprising the enemy.

By the end of 1864, Union forces swept through the South. The Union controlled almost all of West Virginia. The bushwhackers were still raiding and killing, but the end of the war was near.

Civil War Ends

On April 9, 1865, Confederate General Robert E. Lee surrendered to the Union Army at Appomattox (Ap-pa-MAT-ox) Court House in Virginia. The Civil War was over. Soldiers who had fought on both sides came home to a new state. In West Virginia, the Civil War had torn apart families and communities. It would take years for all the hurts to heal.

CHAPTER 10

After the War

Freed Slaves Face New Problems

After the Civil War, thousands of former slaves came into the Shenandoah and Potomac Valleys of West Virginia. They were ready to start a new life. What they found was not what they had dreamed of. They lived in tent camps. Conditions were bad. Disease and sickness spread. Babies, young children, and old people were especially hard hit.

On the plantations, slaves had not learned how to read. They were often punished if they were caught reading, or trying to learn.

Martinsburg, Berkeley County

Charles Town, Jefferson County

Schools for African Americans were set up in the towns in the Eastern Panhandle by the Free Will Baptists. White people who did not want African Americans to have schools threatened the life of a teacher in Charles Town.

African Americans in Martinsburg raised $50 a

month to keep their school open. Whites broke the windows and did what they could to stop the classes.

In the Kanawha Valley, African American preachers raised money from the people in their churches to set up their own schools.

Booker T. Washington

Booker T. Washington, who became a great educator, went to one of these schools.

After the Civil War, the state government passed laws to punish people who had been Confederates. Former Confederates could not vote, teach, hold office, or practice law.

Charleston Becomes State Capital

Charleston, Kanawha County

In 1870, people who had been Confederates were allowed to vote again. Democrats won power in West Virginia. They moved the capital from Wheeling to Charleston. At that time, Charleston was a small village. Within five years, lawmakers changed their minds and moved the capital back to Wheeling. When the people were given the chance to vote, Charleston won.

In 1885, state records were loaded onto a barge and moved back to Charleston for the last time.

State Seal Created

French-born Joseph Diss DeBar became the state's commissioner of immigration. He designed the state seal of West Virginia. On it is a farmer, a miner, and the state's motto, "Montani Semper Liberi." The words are Latin. They say, "Mountaineers are always free."

State Seal, front & back.

Factories, Farms, and Revenuers

Diss DeBar tried to get industry and new people to come to West Virginia. He thought industry would be good for the state. West Virginia was rich in timber, coal, oil, and natural gas. These were needed by a country that was growing fast. In the rest of the nation, many people were leaving their farms to work in factories in the cities.

Before industry came to West Virginia, the land provided the people with most of the things they needed. Whole families worked together to make the best life they could for themselves.

The land and the family were more important than anything else. Men hunted, cleared the land and planted crops or raised livestock. Women took care of the children, tended gardens, and made the clothes. Making and selling moonshine, a whiskey made from corn, was a way the family could earn cash. Life was hard, but few went hungry. Strangers were usually made to feel welcome.

That changed when a federal law was passed to stop the sale of untaxed liquor. The U.S. President, Rutherford B. Hayes, sent federal tax collectors to West Virginia. These tax collectors were known as "revenuers." The revenuers hired people to find the moonshine stills and to spy on their neighbors. Many people no longer trusted strangers.

Building the Railroad Is Difficult and Deadly

In the spring of 1870, workers began to build the Chesapeake & Ohio Railroad into southern West Virginia. This rugged land was probably one of the hardest places in the country to build a railroad. Cuts had to be made through hills. Tunnels had to be blasted through mountains.

Crews trying to lay out the route had to be lowered by rope into some of the steep canyons of the New River. Irish and German immigrants, people who had just arrived in this country, came to work on the railroads. Thousands of freed slaves joined them.

The railroad expansion came at a price. We do not know how many men died while building the railroad. Many men were crushed by cave-ins in the tunnels. Others died in other kinds of accidents.

Workers dug a 6,000-foot tunnel through Big Bend Mountain in southern West Virginia. The hard red shale of this mountain caused many rock falls. The story is told that the bodies of men killed were buried in the pile of rocks and stones outside the tunnel opening. The people in charge of building the tunnel had the bodies buried at night because they were afraid the workers would quit if they knew how many men had been killed. Big Bend Tunnel was completed in July of 1872. At that time, it was the longest tunnel in the country.

Big Bend Tunnel, Summers County

The Legend of John Henry

A legend grew up around one African-American worker who helped dig that tunnel. His name was John Henry. He was a powerful man. With his hammer, he said he could beat a steam-powered drill at breaking through the rock in the tunnel. According to the legend, John Henry beat the steam drill, but the effort caused his heart to burst. Through stories and songs, people all over the world know about John Henry, the man who "died with a hammer in his hand."

CHAPTER 11

Industry Brings Changes

Not everyone wanted railroads. A newspaper in Greenbrier County said the railroad would bring in liquor, put cattle drivers out of work, kill chickens and cows, and scare horses. But there was no stopping it. When it was built, the railroad brought the outside world to an area that had been cut off from it.

Business and Politics Come Together

Henry Gassaway Davis began his working life as a brakeman on the B&O Railroad. During the Civil War he opened up a general store. He made a lot of money selling supplies to the B&O. With that money, he formed a bank and a land company that bought up farmland, timber, and coal. He and another wealthy man, Johnson N. Camden, built railroads into the mountains to reach the coal and timber they owned. In 1871, as a Democratic candidate, Davis defeated Waitman Willey and became one of West Virginia's senators to the U. S. Congress.

Business and politics became tied together. Many members of the legislature worked to pass laws that benefited the companies that got them elected. Business interests controlled the politics of almost every town and county seat.

Land and Mineral Rights Are Bought Up

Industry spread into the mountains and valleys of West Virginia. With industry came people who saw land as something to buy and use in order to make money. They bought up all the land and mineral rights they could.

Mineral rights were the rights to own, and remove, the oil, coal, and gas in the earth. When landowners sold only the mineral rights, but kept title to their land, the sales contract they signed was called a "broadform deed."

Land sold cheaply. One land agent gave people sewing machines in return for their land. Other agents bought land for as little as one dollar an acre. The land was often bought by companies who did not care how they used it, how they left it, or what happened to the people who had lived on it.

Most people who had settled and lived on this land did not realize the value of what they sold so cheaply. They did not understand the broadform deeds that they signed. They did not understand that the owners of the minerals under their land could destroy the top of their land to get the minerals out. They did not see ahead to the drilling platforms, the railroad sidings, the coal-mining buildings, and the strip mines that would tear up and destroy their land.

The Hatfields and McCoys

As the companies were moving in and taking over the land, the rest of the country was hearing about West Virginia. They were reading about the feud between the Hatfields and the McCoys.

Anderson Hatfield was a great bear hunter. When he killed his first bear, he described himself as "fit to face the devil." Maybe his nickname, "Devil Anse," comes from that. No one knows for sure. In addition to being a great bear hunter, Anse Hatfield was also a large landholder in Logan County. Both he and Randolph McCoy, who lived on the Kentucky side of the Tug Fork River, made money selling timber. The feud began when Randolph McCoy's son attacked Devil Anse's brother, Ellison. When Ellison died, the Hatfields captured the McCoys who were responsible for his death and shot them. The feud continued. More people were killed on both sides.

Newspapers covered the story. They exaggerated

Logan County

Devil Anse Hatfield (middle row, second from left) and his family. This photograph was taken in 1897, several years after the feud that made him famous.

it to make it more interesting. Eleven people were killed, but the news stories said that hundreds died. They described the people as hillbillies who carried guns and jugs of whiskey. That was the picture of West Virginians that was given to the rest of the country.

Oil and New Products

Sistersville, Tyler County

Meanwhile, industry was changing West Virginia. Oil was discovered along the Ohio River. By 1893, Sistersville had the largest producing oilfield in the world. By 1900, Wheeling and the area around it had about one-third of West Virginia's factories. Over half of Wheeling's labor force worked at making steel, pottery, cloth, and tobacco products.

Timberland Laid Bare

Another one of West Virginia's valuable resources was timber. Forests that had never been cut covered two-thirds of the state. Then logging railroads were built up into the forests from the main railroad lines. Once again, it was often the immigrants, the people who had just moved here from other countries, who laid the tracks. Logging camps were built in the woods. A crew of six men could cut 200 trees in one day. All of the trees were cut until a mountain was bare.

When the lumberjacks—or wood hicks, as they were called in West Virginia—came to town on Saturday nights, many of them came to drink. Fights spilled out of saloons such as those in Brooklyn across the Greenbrier River from Cass.

Large companies from other states owned most of the timber industry in West Virginia. They bought the best timberland for just two to five dollars an acre. The lumber from a tree that cost them 50 cents often sold for as much as $200.

West Virginians had jobs but these jobs lasted for only a short time. They lasted only as long as the trees.

By 1900, half of the forests were gone. By 1920, almost all of the 10 million acres of tall trees were gone. Fires swept over the mountains. Streams were filled with silt and sediment. The land that was once beautiful and full of life was now ugly and dead.

CHAPTER 12

King Coal

The United States was growing. Coal was needed for factories, ships, and locomotives, as well as for home furnaces. Before 1900, most coal came from coalfields north of West Virginia.

After the railroads were built into the coal-rich areas of West Virginia, dozens of small companies opened up mines. Many of the operators of these mines were former miners from England, Wales, and Scotland. Some of them had mined coal in Pennsylvania, and then moved to West Virginia.

From Small Mines to Big Ones

Most of these early coal operators borrowed money to open up small mines not far from a railroad. The mines were usually far away from towns. The coal operators had to bring in everything they needed, or they had to build it on the spot. Often, one of the first things they built was a sawmill. This supplied them with lumber to build houses.

A lot of men who had worked on the railroad stayed to work as coal miners. Small coal companies also hired local farmers to work in the mines. These men mined only part of the year. They returned home in the spring to plant their crops and in the fall to harvest them. Many of them took off work to go hunting or fishing. Coal operators did not think these farmers were good mine workers.

As the coal operations grew larger, the operators hired immigrants. They came from many countries—Italy, Hungary, Russia, Germany, Greece, and Poland. Also, thousands of African Americans came from the southern states to work in the mines.

By 1900, there were 20,000 coal miners in West Virginia. About 6,000 of them were immigrants, and about 4,000 were African American. Many were native West Virginians who had left their farms.

Coal Camps and Coal Towns

In places where mines were located far away from towns, most of the miners and their families lived in coal camps. The camps were made up of small houses that the operators built near the mines. When mines were small, operators and workers lived together in these camps. When the operators grew richer, they moved their families out of the coal camps.

Coal mining gradually changed from small operations to big business. Due to competition, most small operations were forced to join together

Metal scrip.

or sell out to big corporations. Coal camps grew into company-owned towns. In southern West Virginia, 80 percent of the coal miners lived in company towns. Ev-

erything in a company town was controlled by the coal company. Doctors, preachers, and store clerks were on the company payroll. Company-sponsored baseball teams played each other on Sunday afternoons.

Paper scrip.

Miners often were paid in "scrip." Scrip was the word for metal tokens or paper coupons that stood for a certain amount of money. Scrip could be used only at the mine's company store. The store often charged high prices for food and clothes. Most miners had no choice; they had to buy everything they needed there. Many times, workers were in debt to the company store.

Harsh Living Conditions

In the coal camps that were far away from towns, the railroad was usually the only way in and out. Some coal towns were clean. Houses in towns such as Holden and Gary were well-built, but in many coal towns the houses were shacks that were put up in a hurry. African Americans and immigrants had to live in their own separate areas, often in the most run-down houses. The company owned the houses and set the rent. Coal dust made everything black. Raw sewage polluted the creeks.

Women spent hours every day trying to keep at least the inside of their houses clean. They tended gardens, often large ones. Many kept chickens and pigs in pens. Cows ran free.

The company controlled everything. On election day, workers were sometimes given a list of people they should vote for.

Harsh Working Conditions

Miners were paid by the weight of the coal they

mined, not by the hours they worked. Operators would
often underweigh the coal. Miners were supposed to be

WV State Archives

*Young boys worked
in the mines.*

at least 14 years old, but boys as young as nine worked
in the mines. The boys worked long hours.

Coal mines were the most dangerous places to work
in the United States. From 1877 to 1928, at least 10,000
men died in West Virginia coal mines. No records were
kept on the number of boys who died. Safety regula-
tions were weak and hardly ever enforced. Inspectors
were usually given their jobs because they were friends
of office holders. In the 1890s, Governor MacCorkle
vetoed a bill that would have made safety laws stron-
ger. He said that nothing should burden the coal industry because the good of the state depended on it.

Miners who complained about their working or living conditions were fired. They and their families were thrown out of their company-owned houses. Sometimes, their names were put on a "blacklist." This marked them as troublemakers and no other mine would hire them.

Miners Unite and Strike

Miners knew they could not improve things individually. They learned that if workers joined together in a union they had more power. If the union called a strike, the mine could not operate.

Before 1900, there were small local strikes. In 1902, the United Mine Workers of America (UMWA) called for a big strike in the Fairmont, Kanawha, Pocahontas, and New River coalfields. The strike was for union recognition. About one-fourth of West Virginia's miners went on strike. The companies fought back with injunctions, state militia, strikebreakers, and scabs. Injunctions were legal orders against striking and picketing. The state militia were men called out by the governor to protect company property. They were supposed to keep order. Most often they were used to help the companies fight the unions. Strikebreakers were armed guards hired and paid by the company to keep out the union. A "scab" was the union term for a person who worked during a strike.

The UMWA brought in Mary Harris Jones. The miners called her "Mother Jones." Even though she was in her 70s, she helped organize and lead the miners. She was afraid of no one and the miners loved her.

Work Becomes More Dangerous

The 1902 strike ended with contracts in most of the Kanawha Coalfield but not in the southern coalfields. Many owners found ways around the contracts to increase their profits. If pay was based on filled coal cars, the company just increased the size of the cars. Living conditions were still bad. Working conditions were more dangerous than ever, with cave-ins, slate falls, and gas-filled mines.

Monongah, Marion County

On the afternoon of December 6, 1907, an explosion tore through the Fairmont Coal Company mine at Monongah, West Virginia. Flames and smoke shot out of the ground. The force of the blast blew buildings across the West Fork River.

A total of 361 miners lost their lives. No one knows how many boys working in the mine were killed. The disaster made widows of 250 women. The company gave each of them $150. "Quite a Christmas present," a company lawyer said.

Strikes Become More Deadly

In 1912, coal operators on Paint Creek in Kanawha

County refused to renew the contracts they had with the union. The miners went on strike. In the next valley, Cabin Creek miners joined the struggle. The miners, who often worked 12 or more hours a day, wanted a nine-hour day

Striking miners and their families being evicted from company houses.

and better housing. They wanted to be paid in money instead of the scrip that had to be used at the company store.

The company fired the striking workers. The company wanted order, and said outside people brought in by the union were trying to stir up trouble. The company hired Baldwin-Felts detectives as mine guards. The guards were armed with rifles, shotguns, and machine guns. They threw striking miners out of their company houses and put their furniture out on the road.

The UMWA set up tent camps for the striking miners. Mother Jones, who was then in California helping other workers, returned to West Virginia to help the miners. "There is no peace in West Virginia because there is no justice in West Virginia," she said. She dared the mine guards to shoot her. In August, she led 3,000 miners in a march on Charleston.

Miners shot at guards and at trains carrying strikebreakers. On the night of February 7, 1913, mine guards and a company official got on an armored train called the "Bull Moose Special." As it traveled through Holly Grove, the guards fired hundreds of shots into the tents of sleeping miners and their families. It was a miracle that only one miner was killed. A few days later, miners marched on Mucklow, now Gallagher, on Paint Creek. Twelve miners and four guards were killed.

Paint Creek & Cabin Creek, Kanawha County

Governor Glasscock sent the state militia—citizens armed with weapons—to try to keep order. At least 300 miners were arrested and sent to jail. Mother Jones, now more than 80 years old, was put under house arrest. A friendly guard smuggled out her messages encouraging the striking miners and telling the rest of the country what was happening.

In the tent camps, many people were sick with smallpox, measles, and diphtheria. There was hardly any food.

A Forced Compromise Ends Strike

On March 5, 1913, West Virginia's new governor, Henry D. Hatfield, paid a visit to the area. He was a doctor. He was also Devil Anse Hatfield's nephew. He ignored warnings that he might be shot. Hatfield spent two days in Holly Grove taking care of the sick. He came back to Charleston determined to settle the strike.

Under the terms of a compromise agreement, workers could trade at non-company stores and both the company operators and the workers could have their own people check the weight of the coal that was mined. There were already laws requiring this, but they were not enforced. Miners were given the right to organize, but the operators were not required to recognize the union. The miners rejected the agreement. Hatfield threatened more troops and prison terms if the miners did not accept the compromise. The miners felt they had hardly won anything, but they went back to work. Hatfield freed Mother Jones and the striking miners who had been put in jail.

At the end of 50 years as a state, West Virginia had seen more than its share of bloodshed: first the fighting of the Civil War and then the struggle for the union in the coalfields.

CHAPTER 13

War in Europe, War in the Coalfields

World War I Needs State's Resources

World War I, which lasted from 1914 to 1918, changed West Virginia in many ways. More than 60,000 West Virginians served in the armed forces. At least 200 were army nurses. The war took West Virginians out of the hills and sent them into the world.

West Virginia's industries were needed to win the war. In Wheeling, steel mills worked night and day. Mustard gas and explosives were produced by the new chemical industries in the Kanawha Valley.

Coal was so important to winning the war that coal miners were not drafted. During the war there was peace between the coal operators and the union.

Post-War Union Efforts Begin

When the war ended, John L. Lewis, president of

the UMWA, began to try to get the miners in southern West Virginia to join the mineworkers' union. He especially wanted to recruit miners in Mingo and Logan Counties. These two counties had about one-third of the non-union miners in the state.

Logan County

Mingo County

After the war, the country did not need as much coal. The price of coal dropped. Coal operators wanted to keep coal miners' wages low so they could continue making a good profit. The coal operators were ready to do anything to keep the union from organizing the miners.

Matewan Is Center of Conflict

The union effort in Mingo County was based in the town of Matewan. Sid Hatfield was Matewan's 28-year-old chief of police. Many sheriffs and policemen were paid by the coal companies to work against the union. Hatfield was different. He promised to protect the miners who joined the union.

On May 19, 1920, Albert Felts and his brother Lee came to Matewan with a group of Baldwin-Felts detectives. They spent the day evicting striking miners and their families from homes owned by the Stone Mountain Coal Company. The Baldwin-Felts men piled the miners' furniture out on the roads.

When Albert and Lee Felts and their detectives returned to the train station, they were met by Sid Hatfield and a group of miners armed with guns. When Hatfield tried to arrest the Baldwin-Felts men, they tried to arrest him. Shots were fired. Seven detectives—including both Felts brothers—plus two miners, a bystander, and the Mayor of Matewan were killed. Because of conflicting evidence, Hatfield and the other defendants were found not guilty of causing the deaths.

Murder Leads to Armed Strike

The following year, Sid Hatfield and his friend Ed Chambers were murdered as they walked up the steps of the McDowell County Courthouse at Welch.

"They shot Sid down like a dog," one miner said. At the trial, no one was found guilty. Miners were enraged at the murder of Sid Hatfield. Now they felt they had nothing to lose by joining the union and going out on strike. Many of the miners felt it was time to take up guns to get what they wanted. They wanted the pay and benefits that union miners had won in the northern part of the state. Coal operators brought in strikebreakers to keep the mines working. During the 28 months of the strike, 3,000 striking miners and their families lived in tents along the roads.

Federal troops were called in three times to keep order. In August 1921, thousands of armed miners gathered at Marmet to begin a march to Logan. They were marching to support the striking miners in Logan and Mingo Counties.

Union organizers were afraid that the marchers would begin shooting. They were afraid the march would do more harm than good. Union leaders talked the miners into stopping the march. But then, on August 28, state police tried to arrest some of the miners—not for marching but on some other charge. Two miners were killed and three were wounded. After that, the miners were determined to march to Logan.

The Battle of Blair Mountain

Don Chafin was the sheriff of Logan County. He vowed he would not let the miners go through his county. On August 31, more than 1,200 state police, armed guards, and others, many of them paid by the coal companies, tried to stop the miners at Blair Mountain. The battle lasted for four days and was fought over a 25-mile front. Over 2,000 U.S. troops were brought in, as well as a chemical warfare unit and airplanes with crude bombs. Faced with such a force, and unwilling to shoot U.S. soldiers, the miners stopped fighting.

The "Battle of Blair Mountain" got the nation's attention. People all over the country knew about the striking miners of Logan and Mingo Counties. But none of this attention brought with it the right to belong to a union. By the end of the 1920s, membership in the union had dropped from 50,000 to 600.

CHAPTER 14

The Great Depression
And World War II

In the 1920s, West Virginia began to build better roads. This changed the way many people lived. They moved down out of the hills. Many farms were sold or abandoned. People built houses, schools, and businesses along the roads. Towns and cities grew. People wanted electricity, indoor plumbing, and telephones. Many women began to work outside the home. People began to hope for a better life. That hope ended with the Great Depression.

What Caused the Depression

The stock market crashed in October 1929. In 1930, there was little rain in the country's farmland. With few crops to sell, farms failed. Factories had been producing more goods than people could buy. As a result, many factories and businesses closed or cut back on production. They didn't need as much coal, lumber, or steel. So West Virginia's industries suffered. Many people lost their jobs. Some could not afford to pay back money they had borrowed. Many banks closed. Some people lost all their savings. Almost everyone suffered in the 1930s. Many people grew gardens for food. Some people warmed their homes with pieces of coal they picked up along the railroad tracks.

Tragedy at Hawks Nest

Hawks Nest, Fayette County

WV State Archives

Hawks Nest Tunnel

In 1930, the Union Carbide Corporation began digging a tunnel through Gauley Mountain at Hawks Nest. Part of the New River was to flow through the tunnel to make electricity at a power plant several miles downstream. Men who badly needed work signed up for the job of digging the tunnel.

Most of the 3,000 men hired were African Americans who had come from the South looking for work. The rock they drilled through was almost pure silica. The company wanted the tunnel dug fast. Safety rules were ignored. Wet drilling was not used because it would take longer to build the tunnel. Silica dust filled the air. The dust clogged the lungs of the workers who breathed it in. Over 700 men,

581 of them African Americans, died of silicosis. Many of them were buried in unmarked graves near the opening of the tunnel. This was one of the worst industrial tragedies in U.S. history.

During the Great Depression, most coal miners were either out of work or working only a few days a month. Life in the coal camps was very, very hard. People who had left their farms and people who had come from other countries to work in the coal mines were stranded in the coal camps. They had little food and little hope for a better life.

Arthurdale Is Created

Scotts Run, outside of Morgantown, was a mining region of about 10,000 people. President Franklin Roosevelt's wife Eleanor visited Scotts Run. She told the President something had to be done for the people who lived in Scotts Run and places like it.

Arthurdale,
Preston County

The result of Eleanor Roosevelt's concern was Arthurdale. Arthurdale was the first of more than 100 communities throughout the nation that were started by the government. This government program took unemployed workers and resettled them in homes, mostly in small communities in the country.

Arthurdale was a new community built in 1933 on farmland about 20 miles from Scotts Run. Families were chosen to live there. The government gave them houses. People planted gardens. They shared in the work of farming and dairying. A school and a factory were built.

The land turned out to be poor for farming. No new factories were built because there were no good roads to Arthurdale. Many people said it was a failure, but Eleanor Roosevelt said it was a success. People who had nothing in the coal camps now had homes and a better life.

World War II Starts

On December 7, 1941, Japanese warplanes bombed Pearl Harbor in Hawaii. The United States was again at war. Just as in World War I, West Virginia's mines and factories were needed to win the war. Unemployed coal miners were called back to work. Thousands of men were drafted into the armed forces. Women were hired to keep the mills and factories running. Wheeling Steel made weapons. Chemical plants along the Kanawha River made explosives and man-made rubber.

Altogether, 218,665 West Virginians served in the armed forces; and 5,830 of them died in the war.

World War II ended in 1945. By 1946, union coal miners were again being called out on strikes by their leader John L. Lewis. These strikes made a lot of Americans mad. The strikes hurt other industries that needed coal in order to run.

Machines Replace Workers, Cause Black Lung Disease

By 1950, Lewis had won better health benefits and higher wages for coal miners, but new contracts allowed big machines to be used in the mines. The machine called the "continuous miner" made it possible to mine coal with far fewer miners. Many miners lost their jobs. African American miners were the first to lose their jobs because many companies refused to train them to work the new machines. The continuous miner filled the air in the mines with coal dust—much more dust than was raised by previous mining methods. Many miners became sick with "black lung."

Health and Safety Improved by Law

It was not until 1969 that the federal Coal Mine Health and Safety Act was passed. Ken Hechler was one of West Virginia's congressmen. He added words to the bill that gave benefits to miners suffering from black lung. The words he added also set a limit on the amount of coal dust allowed in mines.

For a while it looked as if the bill would not become a law. Too many coal companies were fighting against it. Members of the Black Lung Association (BLA), an organization made up of miners and former miners, went to Washington. Widows of some of the 78

Farmington,
Marion County

miners killed in a mine explosion in 1968 in Farmington went to Washington. They told the congressmen about the bad conditions in the coal mines. It was their personal stories that got the bill passed. It was a great victory. The law made underground mines safer and healthier.

CHAPTER 15

Sixties and Seventies

West Virginia Helps Kennedy

In February of 1960, a rich Catholic man from the East visited West Virginia. He signed up as a candidate for U.S. President in the West Virginia primary election. He felt that if he could win the primary in West Virginia—a working class, mainly Protestant state—he would have a better chance of being elected President of the United States. The man's name was John F. Kennedy.

Kennedy drove hundreds of miles around the state. He talked to people and listened to what they had to say. In the May primary, Kennedy won. He called this victory in West Virginia his most important step on the way to the White House.

Kennedy Helps West Virginia

After he became President, Kennedy sent government aid to needy families. He approved money to build new highways in the state. On June 20, 1963, he returned to West Virginia to help celebrate the state's 100th birthday. It was raining when he spoke in Charleston. President Kennedy said, "The sun doesn't always shine in West Virginia, but the people always do." When he was killed on November 22, 1963, West Virginia lost a good friend.

In 1964, President Lyndon Johnson declared a "War on Poverty." Newspaper and television people came to West Virginia. They were looking for pictures to go with their stories about the poor. Too often, the reporters showed West Virginians as dirty, barefoot people sitting on broken-down porches. West Virginians have always been proud people. These pictures made them angry.

Surface Mining Increases

More and more coal was being dug from surface mines instead of underground mines. These strip mines needed fewer workers than the old mines. Strip mines also left ugly scars on the land. Water backed up behind gob pile dams. These were dams made of rocks and dirt piled up from the surface mines.

Buffalo Creek, Logan County

The Buffalo Creek Dam Disaster

At the head of Buffalo Creek in Logan County, the coal company had formed a gob pile dam. The water backed up by this dam was used to wash the coal. This dam was not only unsafe, it was against the law. People warned the company and state and federal agencies that the dam might break. Their warnings were ignored.

On the morning of February 26, 1972, the dam on Buffalo Creek broke. A wall of water rushed down the valley. It killed 125 people. Of the 5,000 people who lived along Buffalo Creek, 4,000 lost their homes. The Pittston Company, which owned the dam, said the disaster was not their fault. They called it an act of God. They did not offer to bring in food or put up shelters. Later they were forced to pay $13.5 million to the survivors.

Better Times

In the middle of the 1970s, people in West Virginia began to hope that better times had arrived. The nation's "Energy Crisis" raised the price of coal. There were more jobs. New people were moving into the state. Many West Virginians who had left the state in search of jobs came back home. People were singing the popular song, "Almost Heaven, West Virginia."

CHAPTER 16

Coming Home

A Good Place to Live

Today, West Virginia is a good place to live. Neighbors help each other. If there is a fire, a flood, or illness, people lend a helping hand. People who have had to move to other states to find jobs often come back to West Virginia when they retire. Many young West Virginians who move away come back to raise their children.

West Virginia's population is growing again. New people and new businesses are moving into the state. New kinds of jobs are replacing jobs in manufacturing. Having a good education is important for these new jobs.

In schools throughout the state, students are being taught to use computers. In these days of instant communication, West Virginia's mountains no longer separate the state from the rest of the world.

A Beautiful Place

West Virginia is one of the most beautiful states in the country. It is rich in natural resources. New roads have been built. Every year, more and more people come to West Virginia to ski and to go white water rafting. They come to camp and to enjoy the state parks. More highways are planned. West Virginians need to be careful that the natural beauty of the state is preserved. West Virginia's land and water riches need to be protected now more than ever.

A Place of Many Riches

West Virginia has other riches besides land and water. Since the time when industry came to the state, West Virginia has been home to many different peoples. Families from southern and eastern Europe and thousands of African Americans brought with them their own talents, ideas, and customs. West Virginia has benefited from this rich mix of peoples.

West Virginia has award-winning writers, musicians, and athletes. West Virginia has museums and art galleries. West Virginia has dozens of festivals that celebrate everything from apple butter and ramps to the old-time music, dance, stories, and crafts.

A Place of Pride

Throughout the history of the state, West Virginians have struggled to make a good life for themselves and their families in this hard but beautiful land. They have not given up. West Virginians have good reasons to be proud.

About the Author

Anna Egan Smucker is a writer and teacher. Her first book, titled *No Star Nights,* is a story about growing up in the steel mill town of Weirton, West Virginia, in the 1950s. The book won the International Reading Association Children's Book Award in 1990. *Outside the Window* is the title of her second book. She has also had several poems published.

With her husband, she has written parts of more than 30 workbooks and student texts in the areas of reading and social studies.

She has worked as a teacher, a librarian, and a writer-in-residence, and has given presentations and conducted writing workshops throughout the United States. She is currently teaching at Alderson-Broaddus College in Philippi, West Virginia. She and her husband live in Bridgeport with their two children.